PAT THOMSON

Pirates, Gold, and Custard

Illustrated by
Scoular Anderson

OXFORD

OXFORD
UNIVERSITY PRESS

Great Clarendon Street, Oxford OX2 6DP

Oxford University Press is a department of the University of Oxford.
It furthers the University's objective of excellence in research, scholarship,
and education by publishing worldwide in

Oxford New York

Athens Auckland Bangkok Bogotá Buenos Aires Calcutta
Cape Town Chennai Dar es Salaam Delhi Florence Hong Kong Istanbul
Karachi Kuala Lumpur Madrid Melbourne Mexico City Mumbai
Nairobi Paris São Paulo Shanghai Singapore Taipei Tokyo Toronto Warsaw

and associated companies in Berlin Ibadan

Oxford is a trade mark of Oxford University Press
in the UK and in certain other countries

Text © Pat Thomson 2001
The moral rights of the author have been asserted
Database right Oxford University Press (maker)
First published 2001

British Library Cataloguing in Publication Data
Data available

ISBN 0 19 915953 X

Printed in Hong Kong

Available in packs

Year 4 / Primary 5 Pack of Six (one of each book) ISBN 0 19 915955 6
Year 4 / Primary 5 Class Pack (six of each book) ISBN 0 19 915956 4

Contents

1
The Pirates

"I can't hold her any longer, Mr Mate. The wind's too strong."

"Hold on, boys. We're nearly into the bay. Remember you're the fiercest pirates off the southern shores. You can do it."

"Look!" yelled a small boy. He was clinging to the rigging with his hands and toes. "I can see a way through the rocks."

"Good lad," yelled the Mate. "In we go."

They were safely in the bay. The wind no longer threatened to tear them from the deck. The sea stopped trying to get on board.

A pirate with a black beard and bushy eyebrows slid down the rigging, as easily as a monkey. "Well done, Jim lad," Thunder Jake said in a deep, rough voice.

"My name's Edward," said the cabin boy. He always corrected them but they never remembered.

"Good lad," said another. He was called Silent Tom. This was not because he could not speak. It was because he rarely spoke, preferring to draw his cutlass.

A thump on the back sent the boy staggering across the deck as another shipmate thanked him. "You're a treasure, Jim lad, with those sharp eyes," said Old Silas.

Edward was beginning to feel like a tennis ball when the cabin door opened and a tall man peeped out. He wore smart knee breeches and a stiff ruff around his neck. He looked a little worried.

"I say, is everyone all right?" he asked.

"All safe, Cap'n," answered the Mate, "thanks to young Jim here."

"Well done," beamed the Captain, trying to step out on to the deck. His sword caught across the cabin doorway and the Mate had to set him free. "I think you all deserve some grog."

"I could do with some food," growled Thunder Jake, "though I'll not refuse some grog."

"Of course," agreed the Captain. "You must all be terribly hungry. What's for dinner?"

They all stared at him. The Captain stared back at them anxiously. Then he looked guilty. "Was it my turn?"

The Mate groaned, silently. What could respectable pirates do with a chief like that? He had served Captain Smellgood's father faithfully and the old man had understood that if you feed a pirate properly, he will follow you across the seven oceans.

The old Captain had been a gentleman. When the Queen had been a young girl, he had become one of her Gentlemen Pirates and made his fortune stealing Spanish gold. The Spaniards were always trundling gold across the seas from South America and while they threatened Her Majesty's throne, they were fair game.

The old man had left his ship and crew to his son. A nice boy, but not cut out to be a pirate. The Mate sighed. How could he leave the *Sea Blade*, the finest ship to be hewn from English oak? He couldn't do it.

He sighed again, then noticed Edward was trying to attract his attention.

"'Scuse me, Mr Mate," said Edward. "I put some beans in with the salted pork this morning. Just in case the Captain didn't have time."

Thunder Jake's black beard suddenly parted to reveal white teeth. That was unusual in a pirate in those days, but it was a professional matter for Jake. If he didn't look after his teeth, he wouldn't be able to carry his cutlass between them, keep his pistol in his right hand and still have a hand free for the rigging. "Three cheers for the boy," he thundered. "That boy will be the saving of us yet."

And in a way, he was right.

2
Mutiny

Captain Smellgood went to bed early. He found being a pirate rather tiring. He would drink his cocoa and soon fall asleep.

The pirates, however were restless. They were supposed to sit below, drinking, banging their tankards on the table and singing sea shanties. In fact, they sat around, staring at the deck. Edward started to hum a little tune.

"Quit that row!" snapped the Mate. Then he sighed. "Sorry, boy. Sorry. It's my nerves. We can't go on like this, shipmates."

There were several growls in agreement.

"The Captain's not the man his father was," said Wooden Harry.

"That's true enough," agreed Old Silas. "Why, I remember when the

Spanish warship, the *Dorado*, tried that daring trick in 1558..."

"You're right, Silas," interrupted the Mate, hastily. He knew Silas's tales could take two days to tell. "But what are we going to do about it?"

"I was thinking of retiring," said Wooden Harry, stretching out his wooden leg in front of him, "but I've nowhere to go. Don't know no other life."

"True, true," agreed Silent Tom.

"And I couldn't leave the *Sea Blade*," sighed the Mate.

"Nor me, nor me," the others said, loyal to their ship.

"Though I could be tempted away by a jam roly-poly pudding," admitted Thunder Jake.

They all fell silent, thinking of puddings. Their mouths watered.

It was a dangerous moment.

"Look," said Edward, "let's make two lists, one for good things and one for bad things. Then everything will seem clearer."

"You're a parcel of brains, boy," said Old Silas, admiringly.

"That's true," said Silent Tom and he was so impressed by Edward's good sense that he added, "Very true."

"Have you got a quill pen handy, Harry?" asked the Mate. Wooden Harry had turned a problem into an advantage when he lost a leg to a shark in Carib Bay. He had made a useful little cupboard in his wooden leg.

The Mate took the quill and made two columns. He wrote GOOD first and looked around.

"The *Sea Blade*," said Thunder Jake and they all cheered.

The Mate wrote: THE FINEST SHEEP
EVER BUILT.

"S-H-I-P," said Edward.

"Oh! Aye, lad, you're right," said the
Mate and corrected his spelling. "Next
thing?"

"A good mate," said Harry and the
others agreed.

The Mate blushed and wrote: ME.

"The finest crew on salt water," continued the Mate, feeling generous, and he added: CREW to the list.

This time all the others blushed (except possibly Thunder Jake but with his black beard it was hard to tell).

"Brains on board," suggested Harry, jerking his thumb towards Edward.

"Certainly," said the Mate and wrote: BOY WITH BRAINS.

"A good captain," said Edward.

"What?" roared the others and the Mate wondered whether to cross out the bit about the boy's brains.

"Well," said Edward, "you've all told me horrible stories about captains who flog the crew, shout all the time and then take all the treasure. Captain Smellgood doesn't do that. He treats us kindly."

They thought about this, remembering terrible, cruel captains who had not cared if the crew lived or died.

"Boy's right," said Silent Tom.

They looked at each other and then the Mate nodded and wrote:

Fair Captain

"Now, what about the bad things?" asked Edward. "Let's make a list of those."

Thunder Jake sighed. "Jam roly-poly pudding," he said. "Haven't had one of those for twenty years."

"Treacle tart," said Harry, longingly.

"Yes, and those little fancy cakes

with cherries on them," said Old Silas.
Silent Tom gave a little sob.

"Mother's custard," he said and
blew his nose on his sleeve.

They pretended to look out of the
portholes while the Mate patted Silent
Tom's arm.

"Do you mean it's just the food?" asked Edward.

"Just? Just?" barked the Mate. "It makes life worth living, that bit of custard on your hard tack. A splash of gravy on your dumplings and you could face fifty Spanish ships. What do *we* get? Burnt stew."

"I can stand weevils but I can't stand burnt food," confessed Thunder Jake. "My old dad always made us eat up our dinners, burnt or not. I've never been able to abide it since."

"Good food would make all the difference," interrupted Wooden Harry, "but what's the use of discussing it? None of us can cook."

"I know someone who can," said Edward. "I'll ask Ma to come and join us."

The pirates stared at him. Then they

started to laugh. They roared.

"Bless the boy," chuckled the Mate.

"She's a very good cook," said Edward, going rather red, "and very handy with a boat."

"Handy with a boat!"

They howled with laughter.

"That would be useful in mid-Atlantic," sniggered Old Silas. "We could use her hankies if we needed extra sail."

They all laughed again, punching each other and tumbling off the benches.

"No, no, lads," protested the Mate, "simmer down." He wiped his eyes and tried to look serious. "It was kindly meant, boy, but I doubt your mother would care to join us."

"She might. She misses the sea."

"We'll take her on a nice sail round the bay sometime," the Mate answered. "Now, just you think about it. What would your poor, dear mother do when those cut-throat Spaniards board us, armed to the teeth?"

"The same as she used to do when she commanded the *Fighting Shrew*," answered Edward.

There was silence. Edward could

hear the wind in the rigging and the slap of water. All the pirates were staring at him, mouths open.

Thunder Jake closed his, then opened it again to croak, "Is your Ma Black Eye Susan?"

"I don't think so," replied Edward. "Her name *is* Susan but she has brown eyes."

"You misunderstand me, boy," muttered Thunder Jake. "Black eyes are what her enemies got."

"I never met her," said Wooden Harry in a reverent voice, "but I'd like to."

"Then let's all go and see her and ask her advice," said Edward.

"If anyone can get us shipshape, it's Black Eye Susan of the *Fighting Shrew*," admitted the Mate.

"True," said Silent Tom, fingering his cutlass.

"That's settled then," said Edward briskly. "We'll go tomorrow."

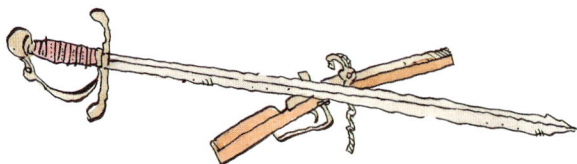

3
Black Eye Susan

Edward's Ma kept a tavern down at the water's edge. There was good food and good grog but no bad behaviour. And absolutely no bad language. The parrot which perched on the barrel in the tap room recited Shakespeare in a very refined squawk.

Black Eye Susan was a handsome, dark woman. She had brown eyes and black curly hair just like Edward's. She was tall and strong and those beautiful eyes could also glitter with menace. She did not mind being called "my dear" in a friendly fashion but the seaman who shouted, "Here, woman, some grog," was likely to find himself sitting in the road without knowing how he got there.

She thought nothing of it when Captain Smellgood and the crew ducked in through the low doorway, but then she saw Edward.

"My own boy!" she cried and he ran to hug her.

"These are my shipmates, Ma," he told her, "and we've a plan to put to you."

"Then come into the back parlour, gentlemen," she answered and soon they all sat sipping hot punch. "Now, will you have a slice of my honey cake?"

The pirates looked at each other as they accepted very large slices.

Thunder Jake closed his eyes. "Ma'am," he rumbled, "they told me I would never get to heaven but at least I've had a taste of it."

"Quite delicious, Madam," said the Captain. "In fact, this unexpected and divinely delicious treat is not entirely unconnected with our visit."

"Get on with it, man," roared Thunder Jake, almost forgetting himself.

"It's like this," said the Mate, hastily, "we're a good crew, with a good ship and very fair prospects of Spanish gold, but we're hungry all the time."

"Sometimes," said Old Silas, earnestly, "I'm so hungry, I can't tell if it's my stomach rumbling or a storm blowing up."

"I've found myself chewing my belt," confessed Wooden Harry.

"By Jove!" gasped the Captain.

"Watch your language," said Black Eye Susan, sharply. "So, why don't you get a cook?"

The Captain, though not a first-class pirate, was a man of some sense. He knew what she was thinking. "No, Madam. We need a fighting pirate who can also put us right on the cookery side, you know."

"I'm handy enough in a fight," replied Black Eye Susan, "but planning is more in my line."

"Planning!" beamed the Mate. "Then you've got brains, like the boy. That's just what we need."

Edward and his Ma smiled at each other. He could see she was coming round.

"I'll do the washing up," promised Old Silas.

"I'll peel the 'taters," said Wooden Harry.

He opened his leg cupboard and took out a potato peeler to show he really meant it.

Silent Tom had been nodding vigorously. Then, suddenly he said, "Mother's custard!" and burst into tears again.

"Quit that snivelling, man," said Black Eye Susan sternly, "or there will be no custard. Where are you going?"

"Back to the Carib Islands, Madam," Captain Smellgood told her.

"Ah, the Islands," she said and she smiled. "My old home. I'd like to go back."

The crew held their breath. A quick movement, and suddenly Black Eye Susan was holding a magnificent sword. Thunder Jake blinked. Old Silas ducked and Wooden Harry fell backwards off his stool. Where had it come from?

"Time to get some practice in if I'm sailing the seven seas again," she said. The blade flashed, a blur of razor-sharp steel. Then she looked down at the precisely and delicately divided honey cake.

"Another slice – to celebrate our new partnership, gentlemen?"

4

The Warship

"Full sail," cried the Mate, happily.

Thunder Jake and Wooden Harry heaved on the ropes, singing heartily, and the extra sails filled with wind.

"We're making excellent time," said the Mate. "Take over, Jake, while I go below."

Everyone was in very good humour, full of rich stew and treacle pudding. Below decks, Silent Tom was stirring

the first custard he had ever made in a
vast cauldron and staring in wonder at
Black Eye Susan's talkative parrot.

"Is this a custard I see before me?"
squawked the parrot.

The Mate smiled as he passed the galley
and went to the Captain's cabin.

"We will reach the Islands today, I calculate, sir," he told the Captain who was embroidering a charming cushion cover.

Black Eye Susan and Edward were studying a large chart.

"We must prepare, then," said Susan. She tapped the curve of the coast. "You say that the *Donna Empanada* will be in this bay?"

"Yes," answered the Mate. "She's one of the boats that take gold back to Spain. She will need to take on fresh water and that is the most likely place. Very quiet and sheltered."

"A delicious spot for a picnic, you know," observed the Captain.

"How big is she?" asked Edward.

"Not so large. She's not heavily armed but she's fast. Quite a small crew."

"A bit like us," answered Edward. "We've only a small crew."

"But we're as brave as lions," pronounced the Captain, sitting up straight, with one hand on his sword and the other on his cushion cover.

"Nevertheless, we only tackle her if she's alone," insisted Susan.

The Mate nodded.

"We'll go in under cover of darkness," Black Eye Susan was saying when a loud cry came from above.

"Land! Land!"

They hurried up to the deck. Edward could see nothing but his Ma was sniffing the air. "I can smell the Islands!" she cried.

The Captain let Edward look through his telescope. Far in the distance, he could see dark shapes like hills rising from the sea.

"Take down some sail," ordered the Mate. "We'd best slow up. Arriving at dusk is best for us."

"Is Dusk near the bay?" asked the Captain.

"I was meaning night-time, sir," explained the Mate, very kindly.

"When it's dark!" exclaimed the Captain. "What a splendid idea. They won't be able to see us! You are so clever, Mr Mate."

Edward sat cleaning his mother's sword, waiting. The sky became darker

and the warm breeze touched his face. His heart was beginning to beat faster but he must stay calm, like Ma. Now he could see the Islands without a telescope. The ship was sweeping round to approach one of them from the opposite side to the bay where the *Donna Empanada* lay.

As they swept softly past, the Captain had his telescope trained on a gap between the reefs. He peered into the bay. Everyone heard him gasp.

"By Jove, it's not the *Donna Empanada*! It's the *Pimento*!"

"But that's a warship with double the number of cannons," said the Mate.

"*Double, double, toil and trouble,*" squawked the parrot.

"You're absolutely right, shipmate," growled Thunder Jake.

5
The Plan

Edward had seen the warship. He had seen the gun ports, the many lights and air of activity. There was no doubt that if she was carrying gold, she was going to keep it.

The Captain, the Mate, Thunder Jake and Ma were sitting round the Captain's table staring at the charts.

"*To be or not to be, that is the question,*" squawked the parrot.

"We mustn't despair, dear hearts," said the Captain. "What was it my father used to say at times like this? KISS, I think."

"Beg pardon, Cap'n?" murmured Thunder Jake nervously.

"Knowledge, Imagination, Strategy – that's planning – and Success, you know."

"Excellent," approved Black Eye Susan. "A man after my own heart. Leave the knowledge to me. Put me ashore tonight and I'll make my way to the village above the bay. I'll find out where the gold is kept for a start."

"Alone, my dear Madam?" The Captain sounded anxious.

Ma smiled. "Don't forget this is my country. I'll be able to talk to people and get all the information we need."

"We'd better take the boat further

along the coast," said the Mate. "I'd like to get some good thick forest between us and the warship. Then we'll get some sleep."

Edward thought he would never sleep while his mother was away but he dozed until daybreak and then worked with the crew.

They spent the day getting the boat into perfect condition and then Thunder Jake made him practise climbing up the side of the boat until he could do it silently. Every weapon was checked and when the Mate at last said, "Time to rest, lads," he was ready to climb stiffly into his hammock and fall asleep.

It was dusk when he woke. He could hear his mother's voice, speaking softly. "There's gold, all right," she was saying. "The *Pimento* only arrived yesterday, fresh from Eldorado. They say the gold is to pay for a new Armada which will destroy the English fleet. There's an admiral on board and the gold is in his state cabin. They set sail in two days' time."

"How many on board?" asked the Mate.

"Only the crew at the moment," Black Eye Susan replied, "but soldiers will be arriving late tomorrow. They are taking them back to Spain."

"So, it's tonight," said Thunder Jake.

"We must consider Strategy now, then," said the Captain.

"You've missed out Imagination," objected Thunder Jake.

Black Eye Susan smiled. "I've made a start on that. I've been cooking all day. My friends in the village are going to invite the *Pimento*'s crew to a great *fiesta* tonight. There will be lots of enticing smells, lots of drink, wonderful music."

"And dancing with ladies?" asked the Captain, hopefully.

"Don't forget, sir, you won't actually be going, sir," the Mate respectfully reminded him.

"They'll leave a guard, of course," continued Black Eye Susan, "but maybe not too many. While the rest of us take on the guards, Harry must row Edward to a small window in the stern of the ship. That's where the Admiral's cabin is. And that's where we'll find the gold."

Thunder Jake grinned, showing his white teeth. "So, while they guard the door and try to stop us getting anywhere near the cabin, Edward will already have climbed inside. And he'll be passing the gold through the window!"

"That's the plan," said Susan. "Can you tell the rest of the crew? I want to get a little sleep."

When they had gone, Edward looked anxiously at his mother.

"Aren't you worn out, Ma?" he asked.

"I'm like a cat," she smiled. "A little

catnap and I'll be ready for anything."
She sighed peacefully as she sank back

and closed her eyes.

The next moment, both she and
Edward were on their feet as a dreadful
cry made the ship's timbers vibrate. It
was clear that something terrible had
happened.

They rushed to the galley where

Silent Tom was sobbing. His weather-beaten old face looked like the afterdeck in a monsoon.

"Is he afraid?" asked Black Eye Susan.

"No," sighed the Mate. "He's burnt his custard."

6
Gold!

The *Sea Blade* was in the entrance to the bay. Two small boats were lowered silently. No one spoke, not even the parrot on Black Eye Susan's shoulder.

A distant sound of drumming came from above the bay where flaming torches could just be seen moving along the cliff edge, as most of the warship's crew set off for the party in the village.

The *Pimento* was also lit up. There

were few lights below decks but shadows could be seen moving in front of the lanterns on the upper deck.

Edward felt as if the surf was crashing against his ribs instead of on the beach. Only Silent Tom had been left on board the *Sea Blade*. He was still mourning his custard but he would have the ship ready to sail at a moment's notice.

Edward and Wooden Harry had rowed the second boat under the stern of the huge Spanish warship, while the others rowed to the front. They would be scaling the side of the tall ship now.

It was time for Edward to start his climb. Wooden Harry tapped his shoulder and then took a strange-looking key out of his narrow wooden cupboard. "Take that," he whispered. "It will open any lock."

Deftly, the old pirate flicked
a rope into the air and
secured it over one of the
elaborate carvings. It hung
just by the only proper
window. That must be
the Admiral's grand
cabin. Edward tied
a basket on a rope
around his waist
and began to
climb.

The window was partly open. He slid his hand inside and pushed it wide open. He tried to swing himself over the sill without making a noise and managed to drop to the floor with only a soft thump. Then he turned and peered into the darkness.

The cabin was the largest he had ever seen. There was a table and some benches. The deepest shadow in the corner must be the Admiral's bed. It even had curtains. No hammock for the Admiral, thought Edward. Ah! By the wall, an oblong, dark shape.

Edward crept towards it and put out his hand. He felt a pattern of brass studs, smooth leather. Yes, here was a lock.

This must be the Admiral's chest. As he put Harry's key in the lock, he prayed the chest was not just full of the Admiral's clothes.

Gold! Edward could see the glint even in the dark room.

He felt heavy bars, bags of coins and shaped objects. He held one shape up to the faintly lit window and saw he was holding a leopard. A golden leopard. This was Aztec gold!

Edward began to fill the basket so he could lower it. He threw down the bags of coins but he did not want to damage the jewellery and ornaments. They were beautiful. There was a snake, studded with turquoise, golden armbands, necklaces and decorated daggers, and they clinked gently as he packed the basket.

Once, he thought he heard something. A snort? He kept very still. He could hear nothing but the hiss of the waves and the murmur of guards' voices outside.

He continued his work. Perhaps the others would not have to attack. He would slip away and no one would realize he had been there until they discovered the empty chest!

Not much left now. Edward picked

up a larger object and held it up towards the window. He found a fierce, shocking, golden face staring back at him. It was an Aztec mask.

It looked like a skull, with gleaming teeth and hollow eye sockets. Edward shivered.

Then he held his breath. There *was* a

noise. He heard a snort, then a mutter. There was someone in the bed and the bed curtains were opening.

7

Two Hostages

Edward pressed himself against the wall of the cabin. He dared not breathe. A man was getting out of the bed. The man came closer. Edward heard a flint strike and, instinctively, he held up the mask to protect his face. In the brief flare, he saw the Admiral gazing at him, eyes wide in horror. Then the Admiral shrieked and rushed to the door.

Edward did not pause. He ran across

the cabin and released the basket. He heard Wooden Harry gasp as it hit the boat.

The rope jerked and dislodged itself and Edward saw that fall, too.

Behind him, two guards came through the door with drawn swords, and in one moment, he was held in a grip that bruised as they pushed him out of the cabin.

The deck was full of armed men. To one side, his head in his hands, sat the Admiral in a nightshirt. Edward looked up and in the flickering light of the torches, there appeared three pirates.

The Mate and Old Silas dropped down to the deck.

"Forward!" called the Captain, elegantly, from above.

"We have the boy," shouted one of the guards. "Surrender!"

The pirates paused.

"For Harry and Saint George," squawked a voice from behind the guards.

They turned swiftly, and in that moment Thunder Jake and Black Eye Susan were there, sliding out of the shadows. Thunder Jake grabbed the Admiral and held his sword to the bewildered man's throat. Black Eye Susan had already torn Edward from the guard's grasp and now stood in front of him, her sword singing slightly in anticipation.

"I say," called the Captain, "my dear Jake, you cannot use a woman as a shield!"

"'Tain't a woman, Cap'n," answered Thunder Jake. "'Tis only the Admiral in his nightie."

Black Eye Susan was speaking to
Edward in a low voice. "Go and get the
boat ready. We'll jump into it."

As Edward ran and jumped and scrambled across the decks, he heard the Captain talking pleasantly. "Now, be good fellows. We don't want to hurt your Admiral, (charming nightshirt, dear fellow, charming) but we are going to take him back with us."

Edward dropped into the boat, fumbled with the oars and got them into position. Old Silas joined him, then the Captain followed, still chatting.

The Mate and Thunder Jake leaped down with the Admiral but the night's events had broken his nerve. The poor man landed in the boat in a tangle of arms, legs, rope and sharp corners. "You're just like a shivering laundry bag, sir," Thunder Jake told him, cheerily.

Black Eye Susan came last, sliding

down a rope. Above her were angry faces, staring down over the side of the ship. They rowed away, hoping desperately that the *Sea Blade* was ready to sail and that the wind would be kind. But as Edward looked back, he saw the *Pimento* lowering a boat.

It was a race. Even if they could get back on board, they needed time to get the *Sea Blade* moving.

"Delaying tactics," shouted the Mate, as they reached the *Sea Blade*.

Thunder Jake tipped the Admiral overboard and then tossed him an oar. "Hang on to that," he said. "Your nightie will keep you afloat until your boat comes."

Soon the *Sea Blade* was moving gently. Everyone was working as hard as they could but they needed to get out of the bay before they could catch

the full power of the wind. Edward and
Thunder Jake watched the Admiral
being picked up. "Oh, good," said
Thunder Jake. "Live and let live, I
always say. When you can."

But the Spanish boat was coming
closer and now Edward saw that the
guards had guns. As he worried, there
was a thunderous BANG. He staggered.
It had been their own cannon firing.

He rubbed his ears and as his hearing returned, he realized that the angry yells of the guards had changed to strange noises which sounded like "Yuk!" and "Eeer."

"Oh, dear," said the Captain. "Not a cannon ball fired in anger, I hope? What happened?"

"'Twas me," beamed Silent Tom.

"Aye, sir," roared Jake. "A terrible secret weapon, he had, sir. He fired his burnt custard at them."

And as they passed out of the bay, the wind filled the sails and the *Sea Blade*, loaded with gold, raced towards home.

About the author

I'll have to be honest, I wrote this story so that I could read it aloud in the classroom in a pirate voice. Try it yourself. It's great.

I'm interested in history, too, and I knew that you could get away with being a pirate in Elizabeth the First's time – if you brought back the gold. I visited an old house where the Tudor owner had become rich as a 'Gentleman Privateer'. Go on, I thought, he was a pirate! So I had the pirates and the gold and, because I used to stay for school dinners, I added the custard.